Who Was Michelangelo?

by Kirsten Anderson

illustrated by Gregory Copeland

Penguin Workshop

PENGUIN WORKSHOP
An imprint of Penguin Random House LLC, New York

First published in the United States of America by Penguin Workshop,
an imprint of Penguin Random House LLC, New York, 2022

Text copyright © 2022 by Kirsten Anderson
Illustrations copyright © 2022 by Penguin Random House LLC

Visit us online at penguinrandomhouse.com.

Library of Congress Cataloging-in-Publication Data is available.

Printed in the United States of America

ISBN 9780399543951 (paperback)   10 9 8 7 6 5 4
ISBN 9780399543968 (library binding)   10 9 8 7 6 5 4 3 2

Contents

Who Was Michelangelo?

A crowd gathered around the new statue in the chapel of Santa Petronilla in 1500. It was indeed a wonder. The sculpture showed a famous scene from the Bible. There was the Virgin Mary, holding the body of her dead son, Jesus Christ. This scene is often called a pietà. (*Pietà* means "pity" in Italian.) Many others had painted or sculpted this same grouping of mother and son. But this statue was different. Although carved from hard marble, it was incredibly lifelike. People could see tiny details, like stretched muscles and the pull of the skin where Mary's hand held onto the body of Jesus. The folds of Mary's gown looked as soft as real fabric. When the sun streamed through the chapel's windows, the statue glowed. It was hard to believe it was carved from stone.

Everyone agreed that it was a magnificent work, unlike anything they had seen before. But who had carved it? Many of the people gathered in the chapel that day didn't seem to know. As much as the crowd loved the image before them, they might not have been looking *too* closely at it.

Nearby, a young man listened quietly. He was amazed that anyone would wonder who the artist

was. *He* had made the statue. Hadn't they seen his name? On a ribbon across Mary's chest, he had carved the words, "Michelangelo the Florentine was making." He wrote "was making" instead of "made" because he had heard that the artists of ancient Greece signed their work like that. It was their way of saying that a work of art was never truly finished.

But Michelangelo (say: mee-keh-LAN-juh-low) was ready to begin working on something new. He had other important projects ahead of him. Soon he would become known as one of the greatest artists in the world. Hundreds of years later, people are still awed by the statues, paintings, and buildings he made.

And he never signed any others. That first pietà is the only one with his name on it. After that, no one would look at his work and ask, "Who made this?" Everyone would know it was Michelangelo.

CHAPTER 1
Education of an Artist

Michelangelo di Lodovico Buonarroti Simoni was born on March 6, 1475, in Caprese, a town in what is now known as Italy. His family was really from Florence, a big city nearby, but his father, Lodovico, had taken a job as *podesta*, or mayor,

Caprese

of Caprese for a year. Then the Buonarrotis, as they were known, returned to Florence.

Michelangelo had one older brother and three younger brothers. His mother, Francesca, died when he was six. The Buonarrotis had once been a wealthy merchant family, but by the late 1400s, they had lost almost all of their large fortune.

Lodovico, though, considered himself a member of the upper class and believed it was beneath him to work. He occasionally took small government jobs, and the family tried to get by on the money he earned from those.

Lodovico thought that Michelangelo seemed clever and decided to send him to school, which was not common at that time. However, Michelangelo became interested in art at an early age, and he spent more time sketching than studying. His father was angry. He didn't want his son to be an artist. He considered artists to be unskilled workers. Lodovico and Michelangelo's brothers often beat him when they caught him drawing.

Italian City-States

RENAISSANCE ITALY

SAVOY
MONFERRATO
ASTI
SALUZZO
MILAN MANTUA
VENETIAN REPUBLIC
FERRARA
GENOA MODENA
LUCCA
LIGURIAN SEA
FLORENCE
SIENA
PAPAL STATES
OTTOMAN EMPIRE
ADRIATIC SEA
KINGDOM OF NAPLES
TYRRHENIAN SEA
MEDITERRANEAN SEA
KINGDOM OF SICILY
IONIAN SEA

When Michelangelo was born, the boot-shaped peninsula now called Italy was made up of independent city-states. Florence, Venice, and Milan were some of the most important ones.

People didn't think of themselves as Italian. They called themselves "Florentine," "Venetian," or "Milanese" to identify their regions.

Most city-states didn't have kings. Instead, they were often ruled by a wealthy noble family. Michelangelo's home city, Florence, was mostly ruled by the Medici family for over three centuries. The Papal States, a group of smaller cities, were controlled by the pope in Rome.

Italy did not become one united country until 1871.

Michelangelo became friends with Francesco Granacci, an apprentice in the workshop of Domenico Ghirlandaio, one of Florence's best-known painters. An apprentice is taught a particular craft by someone who is a master at it, in exchange for the work they do. Granacci introduced Michelangelo to Ghirlandaio, who invited him to become one of his apprentices. Lodovico still didn't like the idea of his son becoming an artist, but he realized that he couldn't stop him. In 1488, when he was thirteen, Michelangelo joined Ghirlandaio's workshop.

Francesco Granacci

Domenico Ghirlandaio

Working with Ghirlandaio, Michelangelo studied the basics of painting, such as how to mix colors and prepare a canvas. Ghirlandaio was working on a series of frescoes at the time. A fresco is a large-scale painting, usually done on a wall or ceiling, that is created by a specific technique using plaster. Michelangelo probably learned how to work in this medium from Ghirlandaio.

Later in life, Michelangelo would say that Ghirlandaio hadn't taught him anything. He even claimed that he had never been Ghirlandaio's apprentice! He wanted people to think that he had learned everything on his own.

But Ghirlandaio had been helpful to Michelangelo. He introduced him to someone important—someone who would change his life.

Lorenzo de' Medici was the most powerful man in Florence. He loved art, literature, and music.

Lorenzo de' Medici

Lorenzo, known as "Lorenzo the Magnificent," knew that Florence had many painters but not many sculptors. In 1490, he asked Ghirlandaio to send over a few apprentices who might be interested in learning to sculpt statues from marble. Lorenzo had a garden filled with antique sculptures for young artists to study, and his staff included Bertoldo di Giovanni, who had been trained by Donatello, the last great sculptor from Florence. Ghirlandaio sent both Francesco Granacci and Michelangelo to Lorenzo.

Michelangelo immediately became fascinated with the art of sculpting and began to visit the Medici garden as often as he could. He made copies of some of the pieces he saw there. Lorenzo the Magnificent was impressed by Michelangelo's work and asked to speak with Lodovico about Michelangelo's future. He wanted the young artist to move into the Medici palace and study sculpture full-time.

But Lodovico didn't want his son to become a sculptor. He thought a sculptor was no better than a simple stonecutter. It would disgrace the family for Michelangelo to make his living that way. Lodovico couldn't ignore a request from a Medici, though, and he finally went to meet him.

Lorenzo said that he would treat Michelangelo like a son and help him become a great artist. In exchange, he offered Lodovico any job he wanted in Florence. Lodovico only asked for a low-level clerk's job. He still didn't believe a Buonarroti should have to work.

Michelangelo was embarrassed that his father did not choose a more important job. Lodovico had missed a great opportunity. Michelangelo was different from his father. He wanted to be important. And he never wanted to miss a great opportunity.

CHAPTER 2
Renaissance Man

During Michelangelo's lifetime, Florence was a center of artistic growth and achievement. At Lorenzo the Magnificent's house, Michelangelo

listened to philosophers and writers talk, and he mingled with other artists. This period of artistic and scientific importance is known as the Renaissance. Life at the Medici home opened up a whole new world for Michelangelo.

In 1492, Lorenzo de' Medici died. Michelangelo returned to his father's house. Soon after that, he was offered a chance to carve a wooden crucifix for a church called Santo Spirito. The church also had a hospital where they treated poor people. Michelangelo wanted to learn more about the human body.

He asked the hospital if he could dissect, or cut open to examine, bodies that weren't claimed by family members of patients who had died, and they agreed. Now he was able to study how muscles connected to one another and how they looked when they were stretched, tightened, or twisted when in motion. Michelangelo used this valuable knowledge to make his sketches and sculptures more realistic.

Florence was supposed to be a republic, a city run by the people. But for decades it had really been ruled by the Medici family. In 1494, the people of Florence rose up against Piero de' Medici, Lorenzo's son. Michelangelo left Florence and went to the city of Bologna. For the next year, he stayed with a nobleman there and sculpted a few small pieces for a local church. When he heard that the Medici family had fled Florence, Michelangelo decided it was safe to return home.

Piero de' Medici

The Renaissance (1300s–1600s)

The Renaissance, a word that means "rebirth," began in Italy in the 1300s. The Middle Ages had been a miserable time in Europe, but then interest in art, literature, music, science, inventions, and architecture started to blossom. People who had become wealthy from international trade and banking—a separate economic and political rebirth—had extra money and time. Many became very interested in the classic art and literature from ancient Greece and Rome. Wealthy families began to collect the works of the great ancient writers and artists.

They also used their money to support living artists, writers, and musicians who were inspired by their rediscovery of these civilizations. Dante, Petrarch, and Boccaccio were some of the great Italian Renaissance poets. Leonardo da Vinci,

Raphael, and Titian were important painters. Great buildings were designed by the architects Brunelleschi and Bramante. People today still study and admire the great achievements of the Renaissance.

The dome of Florence Cathedral
designed by Filippo Brunelleschi

Once back in Florence, he did some work for Lorenzo di Pierfrancesco de' Medici, a less-important member of the Medici family. One sculpture was of a sleeping Cupid, based on an ancient statue he had seen in Lorenzo the Magnificent's garden. Lorenzo di Pierfrancesco suggested that if Michelangelo made it look like an older statue, they would be able to pass it off as an antique and sell it for more money in Rome. They buried the statue to make it look dirtier and older, and then sold it for a high price to a Catholic church official named Cardinal Riario in Rome. When Riario heard whispers that his statue was actually a new sculpture from Florence, he became angry. He sent an employee to Florence to find the artist who had made it. Riario wanted proof that the statue was not an antique so he could get his money back. But he also had been impressed by the statue and hoped to bring the talented artist back to Rome to work for him!

Riario's employee searched all over Florence for the mysterious artist. Finally, he arrived at Michelangelo's house and pretended he wanted to have a sculpture made for himself. He asked the young artist if he could see some work. According to Michelangelo, he did not have any sculptures in his workshop at the moment, so he offered to sketch the man's hand.

The man from Rome looked at the drawing and was convinced that he had found the right artist. Michelangelo admitted that he had made the Cupid statue. When the man invited him to come to Rome, he agreed. Rome was an important city, and Michelangelo knew he would have the opportunity to make his name there.

In Rome, Cardinal Riario gave the young sculptor a block of marble and asked him to carve something from it. Michelangelo spent a year sculpting a statue of the Greek god Bacchus, but Cardinal Riario didn't like it. In the end, it was sold to one of the cardinal's business associates.

Bacchus

Michelangelo looked for more work from the wealthy citizens of Rome, and in 1497, he got his big break. A French cardinal offered him a commission to carve a pietà—a statue of the Blessed Mother and her son, Jesus. A commission is a formal request to produce something, like an order for a piece of art. The patron, or buyer, tells the artist what to make. They sign a contract that states how much the artist will be paid, how long it will take to create, and what materials or other expenses the patron agrees to pay for. Michelangelo's commission even promised that the statue would be "more beautiful than any work in marble to be seen in Rome today." He was that confident.

But his confidence was based on his very real talent. When Michelangelo finished the *Pietà* in 1500, people were amazed. The sculpture was almost six and a half feet tall and six feet wide. Michelangelo had put his knowledge of the human body to work. The body of Christ looked very real. Mary's face reveals deep sadness.

Michelangelo had discovered that he could create soft emotion from the hard marble.

Michelangelo was just twenty-five years old. But he had already made one of the most famous works of art in history.

CHAPTER 3
The Giant

In 1501, Michelangelo heard from friends in Florence that a large block of marble at the Office of Works of Florence Cathedral was available for a sculptor to use. The marble had been brought

to the city about forty years earlier for a sculptor to carve a statue of the biblical hero David. According to the Old Testament story, David kills the giant Goliath with just a small rock flung from his slingshot. But the first sculptor had made a few bad cuts—his own mistakes—in the stone and decided he couldn't use it. The marble had been sitting at the Office of Works ever since. Now city officials wanted a statue that they could place high up in the Duomo, Florence's famous cathedral known for its large dome.

Michelangelo rushed to Florence. Another older, better-known sculptor had said that he could create a sculpture for them, but he would have to add on pieces from another block of marble. Michelangelo said he could make the statue out of just that single block of stone. The officials at the Office of Works much preferred Michelangelo's plan. They agreed to let him carve the statue.

The Art of Sculpting

How do artists turn a big block of marble into a beautiful statue? First, most artists will make a small model of the statue they want to sculpt. In Michelangelo's time, the model would have been made of wax or clay. Next, they might sketch a rough outline of the statue on the marble. Then they use a hammer and a large chisel to hack away all the marble that won't be part of the finished statue. With a fork or claw chisel, artists chip away at the marble and shape the statue. (Most artists use a tiny, flat chisel to create the finer details of their statues, but Michelangelo liked the grooves made by fork chisels.) Finally, they can polish the marble with sandpaper to smooth the stone.

Michelangelo started working on the statue on September 13, 1501. For privacy, he had a wooden shed built around the block of marble at the Office of Works. He worked steadily on the David statue but kept busy with other things as well. Michelangelo began writing poetry during this time. He would continue to write poems for the rest of his life.

Finally, in June 1503, Michelangelo took down the shed so people could see the statue. The committee from the Office of Works looked at the statue and knew they had to change their plans. It was too beautiful, too magnificent to be placed high above the ground, where people would not ever see the detail of its artistry.

David is about seventeen feet tall and weighs around six tons. He stands with his weight on his right leg, with his left leg relaxed in front of him. The rest of his body is turned slightly, and a sling is flung over his left shoulder. In his right hand, he holds a rock. He looks off into the distance, as if he has just spotted Goliath and is

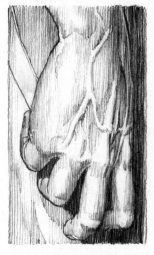

David's right hand

preparing to fight. This pose gave Michelangelo another opportunity to show how closely he had studied the human body. The muscles are tensed in David's right leg, and the skin around his chest and ribs is stretched and twisted, like a real person's might be.

The Office of Works put together a committee of great artists and architects in Florence, including the famed Leonardo da

Vinci, to consider various locations for the statue. They discussed all the different places it could go. Finally, they decided to put it in front of the Palazzo Vecchio, Florence's city hall. Leonardo disagreed

Palazzo Vecchio

with this choice. He was not very impressed by the statue and wanted to put it in a less visible place. He even privately wrote out the details of what he thought was wrong with *David* and then sketched a version of how he would have made it!

To move the giant sculpture, an architect designed a frame where the statue hung from

beams across the top of a platform, so it would not be damaged by bumps in the road. The cart was hauled across temporary wooden tracks laid down for the occasion. It took four days and forty men to move it. People quickly nicknamed the statue *Il Gigante*, or "the Giant." The statue arrived at its new location on May 18, 1504.

Michelangelo vs. Leonardo

Leonardo da Vinci (1452–1519) was considered one of the greatest artists and thinkers of the Renaissance. In addition to creating such famous works as the *Mona Lisa* and the fresco the *Last Supper*, he studied how plants grew and how the muscles and bones of human and animal bodies functioned. He drew plans for flying machines and parachutes.

Leonardo and Michelangelo did not have much respect for each other. Leonardo thought painting was the greatest art form. Michelangelo thought sculpting was the greatest. Leonardo blended the lines of his paintings to give them a soft, smoky look. Michelangelo painted sharp lines and shadows to make his paintings almost seem like sculptures. Leonardo was considered good-looking, and he was well dressed. Michelangelo was not known for his looks, and he wore the same clothes all the time.

They did have one thing in common, though: They both left many projects unfinished!

At age twenty-nine, Michelangelo had already created two unforgettable sculptures that were awe inspiring to all who saw them. It seemed like success had come easily to him. But he was about to take on some of the most difficult projects of his life.

CHAPTER 4
The Painting on the Ceiling

Soon after finishing *David*, Michelangelo was asked to paint a fresco in the Palazzo Vecchio, the city hall in Florence. Leonardo da Vinci had been commissioned to fresco the opposite wall. Many people anticipated the competition between the two great artists!

But neither painting was ever completed. Both sketched cartoons, huge drawings of what they planned to paint. Both showed real battles from past history. Leonardo's was called the *Battle of Anghiari*. He started to paint but gave up when the type of paint he wanted to use for his fresco began to flake off the wall. Michelangelo's was called the *Battle of Cascina*. Many artists admired his cartoon for the lively energy of the

The *Battle of Cascina*

soldiers rushing to battle. They drew their own copies of it. But before Michelangelo could start the fresco, he was called to Rome to work for the new pope, Julius II.

In Rome, Pope Julius II asked Michelangelo to design a giant marble tomb for him. (It was common for important people to plan and build fancy tombs for themselves while they were still alive.) Michelangelo designed a grand, three-level structure with over forty statues around it. The tomb would sit inside Saint Peter's Basilica, the largest church in Rome. And Pope Julius II planned to be buried there.

So Many Popes

Pope Julius II

During the Renaissance, Catholic popes were often wealthy men who came from noble families. They were very powerful. They spent a lot of the church's money commissioning all types of art and buildings. For an artist to receive one of those commissions was a great opportunity.

Here's the list of popes who headed the Catholic Church during Michelangelo's working life:

- Pope Julius II (r. 1503–1513)
- Pope Leo X (r. 1513–1521)
- Pope Adrian VI (r. 1522–1523)
- Pope Clement VII (r. 1523–1534)
- Pope Paul III (r. 1534–1549)
- Pope Julius III (r. 1550–1555)
- Pope Marcellus II (r. 1555)
- Pope Paul IV (r. 1555–1559)
- Pope Pius IV (r. 1559–1565)
- Pope Pius V (r. 1566–1572)

Michelangelo spent months choosing marble for the giant project. But then Julius II decided to focus on rebuilding Saint Peter's, which was over a thousand years old. He told Michelangelo to put the tomb plans aside. Julius II decided that first he wanted painted frescoes on the ceiling of the Sistine Chapel, a chapel that was part of the pope's official home.

Sistine Chapel

Michelangelo didn't like that idea. He preferred sculpting to painting. He didn't even think he was such a great painter, and he didn't have much experience with frescoes.

One day in 1506, Michelangelo went to visit Julius II and was told by his servant that he couldn't see him. Michelangelo was shocked and insulted. Julius II usually welcomed him. Michelangelo, who had a quick temper, decided that he'd had enough. That night, he packed up his things and rode straight to Florence.

Julius II was furious when he found out that Michelangelo had left Rome. He sent messengers to Florence, commanding him to return. Michelangelo stubbornly refused. Florence was an independent republic, and the pope could not force him to do anything as long as he was there. But the messages and threats continued. The leader of Florence became nervous. He worried that the pope might attack Florence! Finally, he asked Michelangelo to go to the pope, and Michelangelo agreed.

Pope Julius II was in Bologna, where he had just conquered the city to make it part of the Papal States, ruled by Rome. Michelangelo met him there, and they made up. However, Julius II now wanted him to make a giant bronze statue of the conquering pope for Bologna. Michelangelo protested that he could not do it. He had only made one very small bronze statue. That had been difficult. Julius II told him to keep trying until he got it right and soon left for Rome. An unhappy Michelangelo stayed in Bologna for two years, working on the massive statue. A few years later, when Bologna won back its independence, it was melted down to make a cannon.

When Michelangelo did return to Rome in 1508, he reluctantly started work on the Sistine Chapel fresco. Pope Julius II had originally suggested a simple design. But Michelangelo had bigger plans. He told Julius II that he wanted to paint stories from the earliest part of the Bible, such as the creation of Earth and humans. Pope

Julius II liked that idea. He gave Michelangelo permission to do whatever he wanted.

The ceiling is sixty-eight feet above the floor of the chapel. Michelangelo designed a type of scaffolding, or platform, high above the floor of the chapel that allowed people to walk below it. He had to climb a ladder just to reach the scaffold platform. Once he was up there, he had enough space to stand as he painted. But it was still very uncomfortable. He had to keep his neck bent as he looked up, and he had to twist and hunch his body to reach some spaces. And Michelangelo still was unsure of his ability to work in fresco. He wrote a comic poem to a friend describing how much pain he was in as he worked that ended with the lines, "I'm not in a good place, and I'm no painter."

After only a few months of work, Michelangelo's worst fears about painting the fresco came true: Mold began to grow on the

part he had completed. He told Pope Julius II that it was ruined and that he had warned the pope that he could not do this. Pope Julius II sent a well-known architect to look at it. He found that Michelangelo had been using the wrong

plaster mix! Instead of firing Michelangelo and giving the job to another artist, as Michelangelo had expected, Julius II just had the bad plaster scraped off and told Michelangelo to start over.

How to Make a Fresco

The art of creating a fresco had to begin the
night before an artist actually did any painting.
First, the area that was to be painted had to be
covered with a thick, rough coat of plaster. That
was left to dry overnight. Next, artists would take

the sketches they had made and pierce the lines of the drawing with a needle, creating tiny holes in the paper. They held the paper against the dried, rough plaster and whacked it with a bag of soot. That left a black outline of the drawing on the plaster, which they then covered with another, very thin, coat of plaster.

Now it was time to paint in color—and they had to work fast! The plaster dried within two to four hours, so artists had to move quickly. They could only finish a small patch at a time, so painting frescoes often took years. And once the plaster dried, it was very hard to fix any mistakes or make changes to the painted fresco. Artists had to be quick *and* careful!

He went back to work and finished the first half of the ceiling in about eight months. Michelangelo needed more money from the pope to continue working, but Julius II was off fighting another war. The artist also wanted to go back to Florence to visit his brother Buonarroto, who was ill.

Buonarroto was the only one of his four brothers that Michelangelo really liked. He loved his father, but they had a difficult relationship.

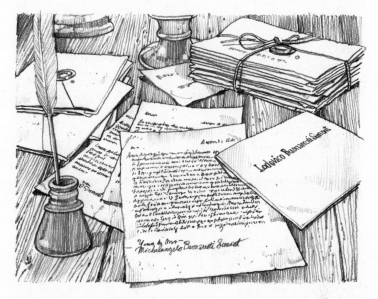

Lodovico often wrote to his artist son, asking for money. Michelangelo wrote angry letters back to his father. He did not have much patience with his family. They needed his money but feared his quick temper. Still, he bought several houses in Florence for them. Michelangelo wanted them to live like the noble family he thought they were.

It took almost a year for Michelangelo to catch up to Pope Julius II and get paid. As he worked on the second half of the ceiling, the pope became impatient. He came to the chapel and demanded to know when it would be

finished. Michelangelo told him, "When I can."
At that time, popes were treated like kings. They
rarely had conversations with common people.
But Michelangelo and Julius II were more
like old friends. Their relationship was not so
formal.

When the completed ceiling was finally
revealed on October 31, 1512, people knew it
was special. Over four years, Michelangelo had
frescoed twelve thousand square feet of space.
His work contained over three hundred different
figures and nine sections that told stories from
the Old Testament of the Bible. It included
God's creation of the universe, the separation
of light from darkness, the creation of humans,
and the fall of humans from paradise. It also told
the story of Noah's ark and the great flood. The
figures were active, energetic, and dramatic. The
colors were bright and rich. The overall effect of
the huge ceiling was stunning.

Michelangelo still insisted that he was not a painter. But he had just created one of the greatest paintings in the history of art.

CHAPTER 5
The Popes' Orders

Pope Julius II died in 1513 at the age of sixty-nine. Giovanni de' Medici was elected as the new pope, taking the name Pope Leo X. The Medicis had taken back control of Florence in 1512 and were once again a very powerful family. Pope Leo X was one of Lorenzo the Magnificent's sons. Michelangelo had known him since he lived in the Medici house as a young man. But Michelangelo

Pope Leo X

didn't think Leo would give him any important commissions, like Julius II had. Leo X was mostly interested in architecture and music, not sculpture. And although Michelangelo had painted the magnificent Sistine Chapel ceiling, a new artist had become a favorite in Rome.

Raffaello Santi, or Raphael, as he was known, was a young painter who had been part of a group of artists hired to fresco the walls of the pope's private apartment in the Vatican palace. His work was so impressive that Pope Leo X gave him more commissions.

Raphael

Everybody loved Raphael. In addition to being very talented, he was charming and handsome.

He was humble and willing to help others. Raphael was outgoing and social. People enjoyed working with him.

In other words, he was the complete opposite of Michelangelo. Michelangelo was considered to be difficult and bad-tempered. He had friends who found him interesting and enjoyed his company, but they were also the kind of people who understood his moods and his dark humor.

It wasn't always easy to be around Michelangelo. Although he earned a lot of money, he bragged that he lived like a poor man, eating little more than bread and wine. In the 1500s, most people didn't bathe more than once a week or  even once a month, but Michelangelo stood out for almost *never* taking a bath. He wore the same clothes for days and rarely took off his boots, even for sleeping. Raphael admired Michelangelo's work, but when Raphael painted his famous *School of Athens* fresco, he included a dark, gloomy figure sitting alone near the center. Many people believed that figure was Michelangelo.

The gloomy figure from *School of Athens*

Michelangelo decided once again to focus on sculpting Pope Julius II's tomb. Julius II had left money with his family for the completion of the tomb, but they thought the original design was too large. The family agreed on a new, smaller design with the artist. Between 1513 and 1516, Michelangelo completed three statues for the tomb. One was called *Rebellious Slave* and another was *Dying Slave*. The third statue was *Moses*, one of the most important figures in the Old Testament of the Bible.

Dying Slave   Moses   Rebellious Slave

Michelangelo's *Moses* is nearly eight feet tall. He is seated but is a powerful figure, with big muscles and an intense stare. He holds marble tablets of the Ten Commandments in one arm. He looks so realistic that supposedly when Michelangelo finished him, he tapped the figure and said, "Now speak!"

In 1516, Pope Leo X surprised Michelangelo by assigning him an important project. Leo X wanted Michelangelo to go back to Florence and

work on San Lorenzo, the Medici family's church. San Lorenzo was a beautiful building designed by the famous architect Brunelleschi. But the facade (say: fuh-SAHD)—the front-facing part of a building—was very plain. Leo X wanted Michelangelo to design a grand new facade for San Lorenzo.

San Lorenzo

Michelangelo didn't want to leave the tomb project again. But he really had no choice. When the pope gave orders, people followed them. Leo X sent Michelangelo back to Florence.

At first, Michelangelo was supposed to work with an experienced architect from Florence. But he thought the architect's designs were boring. Instead, he studied all he could about architecture and began to create his own designs. At the end

of 1517, he had an almost seven-foot-tall wooden model of his design built and sent to Rome. He began to look for marble for the facade.

But then, in 1520, everything came to a halt. Pope Leo X told Michelangelo to stop buying marble. He had lost interest in the project.

Michelangelo was furious. He had spent almost four years of his life in Florence working on the facade project. Now he had nothing to show for it.

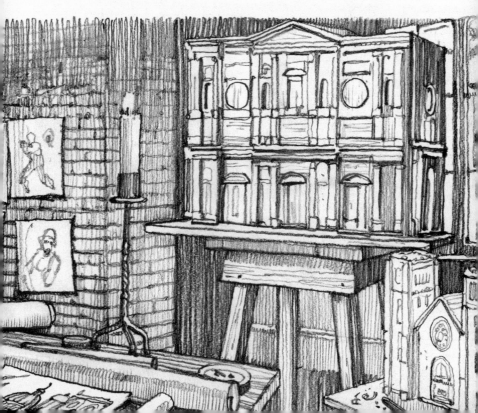

CHAPTER 6
Defending Florence

Although Michelangelo had stopped working on the facade of San Lorenzo, Cardinal Giulio

Pope Clement VII

de' Medici, Pope Leo X's cousin, stepped in with another idea for the family church. He wanted Michelangelo to build a new sacristy— an area where a priest prepares for mass. The chapel already had one, but the cardinal wanted a matching one on the other side of the building. The new sacristy would also include tombs for several members of the family, along with a number of statues. Michelangelo began to work on plans for the new building.

In 1523, Cardinal Giulio de' Medici was elected pope. He took the name Pope Clement VII. Clement VII loved art and was always interested in Michelangelo's ideas and designs. They had known each other since Michelangelo was a student in Lorenzo's sculpture garden. Michelangelo and Clement VII could talk to each other almost like equals.

Clement VII gave Michelangelo more money for the Medici Chapel project. He also told him to begin work on a new library for the Medici family's collection of books.

Michelangelo set up a large workshop in Florence, where he took charge of a group of stone carvers. He made detailed wooden models of the buildings he designed and outlines for the stone carvers to follow.

At night, after the workers were gone, Michelangelo worked on clay or wax models for the statues he planned to carve. He considered himself a "night person" and often worked late. For light, he wore a hat made of thick paper with a candle set in the middle of it. That allowed him to see what he was doing while keeping his hands free.

It seemed like Michelangelo should have been able to just focus on the Medici projects for the next few years. But in 1526, Pope Clement VII led several Italian city-states and France to war against the Holy Roman Empire and Spain.

The Holy Roman Empire included parts of what are now the countries of Germany, Austria, Poland, Italy, and France. As the war dragged on, the people of Florence saw a chance to take back their city from the Medicis. In 1527, the Florentines pushed out the Medici family ruler and organized a new government. Florence became a republic again.

The leaders of the new Florentine republic asked Michelangelo, who was by this time very well known, to design structural defenses to protect Florence. He drew plans for strengthening the walls around the city, then oversaw the building of them.

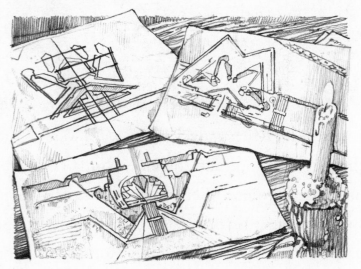

Michelangelo's plans for the walls of Florence

In 1529, Michelangelo's city walls were put to
the test. The pope and the Holy Roman emperor
had agreed to end their war against each other.
But the war wasn't over for Florence. The pope
had made a deal with the Holy Roman emperor.

The emperor would use his large army to take back Florence for the Medici family.

The army camped outside of Florence and then attacked. Heavy cannonballs flew directly into the bell tower of the church of San Miniato.

But Michelangelo had made sure the building was ready. He had bales of hay and straw-stuffed mattresses lowered from the top of the tower. They hung around the building and blunted the blows of the cannonballs. The tower survived the attacks.

Michelangelo's defenses held up well. But the emperor's army had another way to fight: It kept people from entering or exiting the city. That meant farmers from the countryside couldn't bring in food to sell. The people of Florence began to starve. It was too much. Florence surrendered in August 1530. The republic was over.

CHAPTER 7
The Medici Chapel

Michelangelo was worried. He had helped in the fight against the Medicis. He knew he could be in trouble. To stay safe, he went into hiding in a secret room in the Medici Chapel. He stayed there for a few months, keeping busy by sketching on the walls.

But Pope Clement VII had no plans to punish Michelangelo. He just wanted the chapel and the library finished. He sent word that it was safe for Michelangelo to return to work. So Michelangelo did just that. But he told a friend that he was now working on the project more out of fear than of love.

And he was still worried about Pope Julius II's tomb. It had been twenty-five years since he had started the project! In 1532, Pope Clement VII helped make a deal with Pope Julius II's family. Michelangelo would finish up the statues he had made so far. Other artists would make five additional statues to finish the tomb.

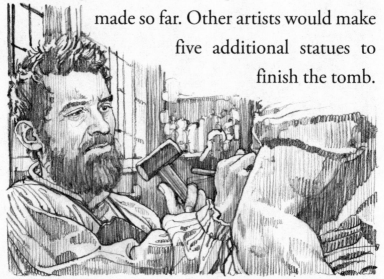

Michelangelo spent the next few years traveling between Florence and Rome. He oversaw the construction of the chapel and library in Florence and worked on the statues for Julius II's tomb in Rome. Then, in late 1533, Pope Clement VII talked him into painting a new mural on a wall in the Sistine Chapel. It would show the "Last Judgment," an important event in the Bible. Michelangelo agreed to take on the new project. But Pope Clement VII didn't live to see it. He became ill in the summer of 1534. Michelangelo traveled to Rome in September. Two days after he arrived, Clement died.

Michelangelo was nearly sixty. He would never again return to Florence. Alessandro, the latest Medici ruler of the city, did not like the artist. Michelangelo had been

Alessandro de' Medici

safe while the pope was alive. But now he had no protector.

The San Lorenzo projects were not finished. Only two of Michelangelo's statues had been put in their places in the new Medici Chapel. One was for the tomb of Lorenzo de' Medici, Duke of Urbino. It shows a man in armor, wearing a fancy helmet. He rests his chin on his hand, as if he is thinking. Across from Lorenzo is the

Statue for the tomb of Lorenzo de' Medici in San Lorenzo

tomb of Giuliano de' Medici, Duke of Nemours. He also wears armor but sits upright, as if ready for action. The statues looked nothing like the real men. They are much more heroic. But Michelangelo did that on purpose. He wanted to show them as they would like to be seen. He said that in a thousand years, no one would remember what they really looked like.

Later, other artists moved the rest of Michelangelo's statues into place. Two statues are at Lorenzo's feet: a woman called *Dawn* and a man called *Dusk*. Beneath Giuliano, there are two other sculptures: a woman called *Day* and a

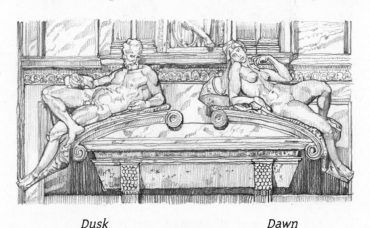

Dusk   *Dawn*

man called *Night*. These four statues were meant to show the passage of time.

Michelangelo left one more complete statue for the chapel, the *Medici Madonna*. It shows the Virgin Mary holding the baby Jesus. But Michelangelo never saw any of these statues— or the completed building—again.

Medici Madonna

CHAPTER 8
The *Last Judgment*

In Rome, Michelangelo settled into the house that Pope Julius II had given him long ago. Over the years, he had earned enough money to live a comfortable life. He was a famous sculptor now, and he even dressed more like a noble gentleman than a poor artist. He had a few servants and assistants who were like family to him. He had plenty of friends in Rome, too, and was especially close to Vittoria Colonna, a wealthy widow. Like Michelangelo, she took her Catholic faith very seriously.

Vittoria Colonna

They had long discussions about their faith and wrote poems for each other.

After Pope Clement VII's death, Michelangelo thought he was free. Surely he would no longer have to paint the *Last Judgment* wall fresco. That had been Clement VII's project. Now he finally could work on Pope Julius II's tomb.

But the new pope—Paul III—told Michelangelo that he wanted him to paint the fresco. So in April 1535, Michelangelo started preparing the chapel wall.

Michelangelo began to paint in May 1536. The wall was about 1,700 square feet. It was smaller than the ceiling, but in some ways, it was more difficult. The ceiling had beams running across it that divided the surface. The wall was just one big, empty space. And Michelangelo was now over sixty. The work was difficult for him.

In October 1541, the fresco was finally
finished. At last, people were allowed to see it.
Many were impressed by Michelangelo's work. It
was a very detailed and powerful image. But some
viewers were shocked.

The Last Judgment is an important moment for Christians. The Bible says it is when the dead will be brought back to life on Earth. Then God will raise some people to heaven and send others to hell. In Michelangelo's fresco, almost everyone was naked. They had huge muscles. These were the kinds of bodies that Michelangelo liked to sculpt in marble.

Some people thought the fresco was brilliant. Some religious people were beginning to say that naked bodies were sinful. They shouldn't be seen this way, in paintings in the chapel. Times were changing. And Pope Paul III had built a new chapel. He wanted Michelangelo to paint frescoes on the walls of what he called the "Pauline Chapel."

Pope Julius II's family had agreed that Michelangelo would only have to sculpt three statues for Julius II's unfinished tomb. One of the statues had to be Moses. Michelangelo had completed that years earlier, and everyone agreed that it was a masterpiece. Michelangelo offered to sculpt two new statues, of Rachel and Leah, women from the Old Testament of the Bible. He finished the new statues in less than a year. The tomb itself was completed in 1545. Pope Julius II's tomb was finally done. Michelangelo had sketched his first plans for it in 1505, forty years earlier. The design had been changed many times. The contract had been negotiated again and again. But, at last, it was finished.

Statues *Rachel* and *Leah*

The artist had completed the statues while beginning work on the frescoes for the Pauline Chapel. On one wall, he painted a scene from the Bible called the *Conversion of Saint Paul.* The other fresco showed the crucifixion of Saint Peter, another Bible scene. Michelangelo finished them in late 1550. He was almost seventy-five years old, and the work had been exhausting. They were his last paintings.

Michelangelo finishes the *Conversion of Saint Paul*

Pope Paul III had died in November 1549, right before the frescoes were completed. But Michelangelo wasn't finished working for him. In

1546, the pope had given Michelangelo another task: He wanted the sculptor to take over the rebuilding of Saint Peter's Basilica—one of the most important churches in Catholic history. It had been built in the fourth century. Pope Julius II had ordered it to be rebuilt back in the early 1500s. Since then, several architects and artists had worked on the project. Even Raphael had drawn designs for it. But it was a massive project. Pope Paul III had put Michelangelo in charge.

Saint Peter's Basilica

After Paul III's death, the new pope, Julius III, had Michelangelo continue to work on Saint Peter's.

Michelangelo changed some parts of the design. He made it smaller, simpler, and stronger. He made sure there would be plenty of light. It would take almost a hundred more years to finish Saint Peter's Basilica. Other architects would make their changes, too. But Michelangelo's designs are an important part of the final building.

The church wasn't Michelangelo's only architectural project. He also designed a building for Pope Paul III's family. He drew plans for a town square and a gate in one of Rome's walls. But even after all this, Michelangelo didn't really

consider himself an architect. On one of his drawings for Saint Peter's, he wrote, "It is not my profession."

CHAPTER 9
A True Master

Around 1547, Michelangelo began to carve a new sculpture. It showed the Virgin Mary and Jesus Christ, along with Nicodemus, another figure from the Bible. He worked on it for eight years, until 1555. Then, one day, Michelangelo took a mallet and attacked the sculpture. Parts of it broke off. His assistant asked him why he had done it. Michelangelo said that he did it out of grief at the death of Urbino, a beloved assistant. There was another reason, though: He had found a flaw in the marble. He didn't think it was worth finishing.

Michelangelo had wanted to destroy the statue completely. But a banker friend offered to buy it. Michelangelo's assistant repaired it and completed it as best he could. The statue became known as

Full *Florentine Pietà*

the *Florentine Pietà*. Many believe that the figure of Nicodemus is a self-portrait by Michelangelo.

Urbino wasn't the only person Michelangelo had lost. Many of his friends had died. So had his father and brothers. His closest living relatives were his favorite brother Buonarroto's children, Lionardo and Francesca.

Other popes came and went. Religious leaders became stricter. In January 1564, a religious council agreed that the *Last Judgment* showed too many naked bodies. They hired other artists to paint clothes on some of the figures.

Michelangelo was very old, but he could never let himself stop working. He had begun to carve another pietà in the early 1550s. He was still working on it in February 1564 when he fell ill. He died on February 18, a few weeks before his eighty-ninth birthday.

Many artists and friends came to his funeral in Rome. He was buried in the Santi Apostoli church there. Pope Pius IV talked about building a much fancier tomb for Michelangelo. But that would never happen.

Duke Cosimo de' Medici ruled Florence at that time. He was furious that Michelangelo had been buried in Rome. Michelangelo was one of history's greatest artists. And he was from

Florence! The duke thought the great artist's body belonged in his hometown.

Michelangelo's nephew went to Rome. He secretly had the artist's body taken from Santi Apostoli. Then he smuggled it out of the city in a bale of hay.

On March 11, the people of Florence packed the streets as Michelangelo's coffin was carried to the church of Santa Croce. There, his body was finally laid to rest, not far from the house where he had grown up.

Today, Michelangelo lives on through his statues, his paintings, and his poetry. He is a giant of the Renaissance who set a new standard for painting and sculpture. Each year, thousands of people travel to Italy to see his masterpieces. They marvel at the *Pietà* in Rome and the giant statue *David* in Florence. Visitors to the Sistine Chapel gaze up at the magnificent ceilings. The image he created of God bringing Adam to life with the touch of his finger is one of the most well-known images in the world. And it was created by a man who said he was not a painter.

Michelangelo always called himself a sculptor. He felt it was his calling to wrestle life from cold, hard blocks of marble. He was never quite able to do that. But he came as close as he could. Michelangelo's statues and frescoes might not be alive, but he lives on through them.

Cleaning the Sistine Chapel

By the 1970s, Michelangelo's Sistine Chapel frescoes were over four hundred years old. And they were covered in dirt. People had been burning candles in the chapel for centuries. That left a coating of dark soot and wax on the magnificent ceiling frescoes. And the plaster was cracking in some areas.

Art experts began to make a plan for cleaning

the frescoes. They knew it had to be done carefully. They wanted to remove the dirt but not change Michelangelo's work in any way. The cleaning process began in 1980. It wasn't finished until 1994.

Visitors were astonished by the change. Colors that had once seemed pale and soft were now deep and rich. The whole ceiling looked much brighter.

Some critics said that the cleaning went too far. But most agree that the original beauty of the paintings has been restored.

Timeline of Michelangelo's Life

1475 — Born on March 6 in the town of Caprese, near the city-state of Florence

1488 — Joins workshop of Domenico Ghirlandaio

1490 — Moves to the house of Lorenzo de' Medici to study sculpture

1497–1500 — Works on the *Pietà* for French Cardinal Jean de Bilhères de Lagraulas

1501–1504 — Carves *David* statue in Florence

1505 — Travels to Rome to build tomb for Pope Julius II

1506 — Asked by Pope Julius II to paint the ceiling of the Sistine Chapel

1513–1516 — Paints fresco on the ceiling of the Sistine Chapel

1508–1512 — Works on statues for Pope Julius II's tomb, including *Moses*

1516 — Hired to build facade for San Lorenzo, the Medici Chapel

1519 — Asked to build new sacristy for the Medici Chapel and a Medici library

1534 — Leaves Florence for good to live in Rome

1535 — Begins work for the *Last Judgment* fresco in the Sistine Chapel

1564 — Dies on February 18 in Rome

Timeline of the World

1472	The city of Amsterdam bans snowball fights
1483	Religious reformer Martin Luther is born in Eisleben, Germany
1485	A solar eclipse is visible in northern South America and Central Europe
1498	Leonardo da Vinci completes *Last Supper* fresco
1509	Henry VIII becomes king of England
1513	Juan Ponce de León becomes the first European to reach Florida
1514	Nicolaus Copernicus publishes his theory of a sun-centered universe
1517	Martin Luther posts his Ninety-five Theses, beginning the Protestant Reformation
1519	Leonardo da Vinci dies
1524	Explorer Giovanni da Verrazzano becomes the first European to see the island of Manhattan
1536	Anne Boleyn, the queen of England, is beheaded
1550	Chocolate is introduced in Europe
1556	An earthquake strikes the Shaanxi province in China, killing about 830,000 people
1564	Playwright William Shakespeare is baptized on April 26

Bibliography

Gayford, Martin. *Michelangelo: His Epic Life*. New York: Penguin, 2013.

Harris, Dr. Beth, and Dr. Steven Zucker. "Michelangelo: Sculptor, Painter, Architect and Poet." *Smarthistory*. August 9, 2015. https://smarthistory.org/michelangelo-sculptor-painter-architect-and-poet/.

Korey, Alexandra. "Michelangelo's Medici Chapel: Light as Symbolic Element." *ArtTrav: Life, Art, and Travel in Italy*. February 20, 2019. https://www.arttrav.com/florence/michelangelo-medici-chapel/.

"Medici Chapels and Church of San Lorenzo." *The Museums of Florence: Art, History, Collections*. Accessed October 6, 2021. http://www.museumsinflorence.com/musei/Medici_chapels.html.

Vasari, Giorgio. *Lives of the Most Eminent Painters, Sculptors, & Architects*. Vol. 9. (Translated by Gaston Du C. de Vere.) London: Phillip Lee Warner, Publisher to the Medici Society, 1915.

Wallace, William. *Michelangelo: The Artist, the Man, and His Times*. New York: Cambridge University Press, 2010.

Website

www.michelangelo.net